Sports Illustrated

1990

25TH SWIMSUIT ANNIVERSARY DIARY

Published by
SPORTS ILLUSTRATED,
a division of The Time Inc.
Magazine Company.

Printed in Japan by
Dai Nippon Printing Company.

Produced by Tom Ettinger,
Director, Sports Illustrated Enterprises

Design by Hopkins / Baumann
Art Director: Will Hopkins
Associate Art Director: Robert Lesser

ISBN 0-316-80731-1

SPORTS ILLUSTRATED
is a registered mark of
The Time Inc. Magazine Company.

North American Distributors,
Book Trade:
Little, Brown & Company Publishers
34 Beacon Street
Boston, MA 02108

Gift and Card Trade:
Renaissance Greeting Cards
Lower Main Street
Sanford, ME 04073

Cover:
Stephanie Seymour
Photograph by
Marc Hispard

Title page:
Rachel Hunter
Photograph by
Marc Hispard

Introduction page:
Kara Young
Photograph by
Marc Hispard

Scenes from
behind and in front of the camera during
the making of the **Sports Illustrated**
25th Anniversary Swimsuit Issue featuring
Carol Alt, Christie Brinkley,
Kelly Emberg, Estelle LeFebure, Maria Von Hartz,
Rachel Hunter, Kathy Ireland,
Elle Macpherson, Ashley Richardson,
Stephanie Seymour,
Yvette and Yvonne Sylvander,
and Kara Young
with comments by
Jule Campbell, Senior Editor.

DECEMBER / JANUARY

S	M	T	W	T	F	S
	1	2	3	4	5	6
7	8	9	10	11	12	13
14	15	16	17	18	19	20
21	22	23	24	25	26	27
28	29	30	31			

SUNDAY 31

214 lbs - up 3 from late dinner.
4.2/30:06 Nordi.TraK - 19.3/Dec 26.3/Yr in 9 sessions.
Exercycle - 11K in 4 sessions. - Basement Stairs - 20x/5:52
Full weight workout - 12x in 1989, but some incidentals
not recorded.
Bicycling - 1140K   4½ mile wogging
32:24 practice in Dec.

MONDAY 1

New Year's Day 213 lbs
Nordi.TraK - 3.0 K in 20:13 - Skis - 2½ to 3 arms 1 to 1½

1:20 P

TUESDAY 2

214 lbs
Full weight workout - basic single 12's - double curl and press.
52 minutes

-1000 cal   1:26 P

WEDNESDAY 3

213 lbs   3.0 K N.T.   3 - 1½ phone interruption
20:26 - 9 AM.
Tried metronome for last 5 minutes - briefly at 90, then at
85

THURSDAY 4

210 lbs   no exercise

1:18 P.

FRIDAY 5

210 lbs.   single 12 weights · double curl + press.
3:0 N.T. in 20:36   3½ - 1   m.m. = 80

1:39 P.

SATURDAY 6

211 lbs   3.7 NT - 30:00   3½ - 1¼   mm = 70
12.7 wK
3x weights   4x N.T.

1:40 P = 10:16 wK   8:58 mo

Stephanie on the rocks in Mexico.
Photograph by Marc Hispard.

JANUARY

S M T W T F S
1 2 3 4 5 6
7 8 9 10 11 12 13
14 15 16 17 18 19 20
21 22 23 24 25 26 27
28 29 30 31

SUNDAY

7

211 lbs   1.5 N.T.   11:14 mm = 72   3½ - 1¼

12× weights - double curl press, + legs - about 1:05-1:10
walk via steps to Bloor Jane + across bridge.

MONDAY

8

1:30 p
210 lbs

TUESDAY

9

1:30 p   -1800 cal
210 lbs

WEDNESDAY

10

1:40 p   0 cal
208 lbs

THURSDAY

11

1:27 p   -500 cal
208

FRIDAY

12

1:00 p   0 cal - wash
207
walk to subway

SATURDAY

13

1:16 p   -2000 cal
208
Fast walk to Runnymede Theatre (19 min)

1:15 = 9:38 wk = 18:36 mo   -2000 cal = 8150 wk

Kathy warms up the beach at Cabo San Lucas.

Photograph by Paolo Curto.

JANUARY

S	M	T	W	T	F	S
	1	2	3	4	5	6
7	8	9	10	11	12	13
14	15	16	17	18	19	20
21	22	23	24	25	26	27
28	29	30	31			

SUNDAY
14

206
Leisurely walk to feed ducks (3 mi)

1:42 p   −1500 cal.

MONDAY
Martin Luther King, Jr.'s Birthday
15

TUESDAY
16

WEDNESDAY
17

THURSDAY
18

FRIDAY
19

SATURDAY
20

Fun and flippers for Kelly.
Photograph by Paolo Curto.

JANUARY

S M T W T F S
1 2 3 4 5 6
7 8 9 10 11 12 13
14 15 16 17 18 19 20
21 22 23 24 25 26 27
28 29 30 31

SUNDAY
21

MONDAY
22

TUESDAY
23

WEDNESDAY
24

THURSDAY
25

FRIDAY
26

SATURDAY
27

Elle puts the "swim" in swimsuit.
Photograph by Jay Maisel.

January/February

S M T W T F S
1 2 3
4 5 6 7 8 9 10
11 12 13 14 15 16 17
18 19 20 21 22 23 24
25 26 27 28

SUNDAY
28

MONDAY
29

TUESDAY
30

WEDNESDAY
31

THURSDAY
1

FRIDAY
2

SATURDAY
3

Elegance on location: Old sneakers and plastic protect Rachel for a trip through the brush.

Photograph by Ann Gallagher.

FEBRUARY

S	M	T	W	T	F	S
				1	2	3
4	5	6	7	8	9	10
11	12	13	14	15	16	17
18	19	20	21	22	23	24
25	26	27	28			

SUNDAY

4

MONDAY

5

TUESDAY

6

WEDNESDAY

7   197 - upper body light workout - 25+10 sit ups.
walk to Jane subway via parking lot - 3 (2+1) sets of stairs at
Faculty.

- 1530 cal   1:30 8.

THURSDAY

8

FRIDAY

9

SATURDAY

10

A giant step for Ashley.

Photograph by Marc Hispard.

FEBRUARY

S M T W T F S

S	M	T	W	T	F	S
				1	2	3
4	5	6	7	8	9	10
11	12	13	14	15	16	17
18	19	20	21	22	23	24
25	26	27	28			

SUNDAY 11

196   4×4 pushups   20×8 situps
35 min walk - P.L. stairs to Jane + Bloor

MONDAY 12

Lincoln's Birthday 196
1 mile run in 12:58 - river - walk at each quarter: 10:30 AM
¼ - 2:31 ½ - 6:13   23:00± total.   33°

TUESDAY 13

196
25 situps 3 pushups

WEDNESDAY 14

Valentine's Day 196
5 Push-ups 17 + 23 s.T ups
1 mile run in 13:14 - river - walks at quarter - 24° some ice
25:00 total 2:55½ 6:21½

THURSDAY 15

197

FRIDAY 16

195 morning pulse - 50
6 Push-ups, 20 situps - strenuous upper body
workout.

SATURDAY 17

"God is in the details." -Mies van der Robe

Photograph by Ann Gallagher.

FEBRUARY

S M T W T F S
                1 2 3
4 5 6 7 8 9 10
11 12 13 14 15 16 17
18 19 20 21 22 23 24
25 26 27 28

SUNDAY

18

MONDAY *President's Day*

19

TUESDAY

20

WEDNESDAY

21

THURSDAY *Washington's Birthday*

22

FRIDAY

23

SATURDAY

24

192   1 mile - inner - 250 - windy - icy, rough footing
      3:05 - 6:31 - 10:01 - 13:30 - walk after each quarter
6+4 pushups - 15+8 situps - dumbell upper body.

3 miles/mo

Estelle looks twice as nice poolside in Huatulco, Mexico.

Photograph by Marc Hispard.

FEBRUARY/MARCH

S	M	T	W	T	F	S
				1	2	3
4	5	6	7	8	9	10
11	12	13	14	15	16	17
18	19	20	21	22	23	24
25	26	27	28	29	30	31

SUNDAY
25
193 1m around block 11:13 4:13 first loop
two walks 050 - light snow.

MONDAY
26

TUESDAY
27
192 1 mile in Hart House. 11:46 non stop.
7 pushups, 20 situps - light upper body.
5 miles jogging in Feb.

WEDNESDAY *Ash Wednesday*
28

THURSDAY
1
190 1 mile 11:13 around block non stop
20°. Bench presses & curls.

FRIDAY
2
189 1 mile 11:09 around block 32°. 2/wk

SATURDAY
3

White is right on Stephanie.

Photograph by Marc Hispard.

MARCH

S	M	T	W	T	F	S
					1	2	3
4	5	6	7	8	9	10
11	12	13	14	15	16	17
18	19	20	21	22	23	24
25	26	27	28	29	30	31

SUNDAY
4
1¾ mile (21 minutes - victoria - around campus
3¾ mo   8¾ yr

MONDAY
5
2 m (24 min) Victoria - on path
5¾ mo

TUESDAY
6

WEDNESDAY
7
2¼ run (27 min) Victoria
8 mo   13 yr

THURSDAY
8

FRIDAY
9

SATURDAY
10

Elle in front of a screen on Lizard Island, Australia.

Photograph by Jay Maisel

MARCH

S M T W T F S
1 2 3
4 5 6 7 8 9 10
11 12 13 14 15 16 17
18 19 20 21 22 23 24
25 26 27 28 29 30 31

SUNDAY
11

MONDAY
12

TUESDAY
13
198
1 mile river - from house 13:07 3:17 to path

WEDNESDAY
14
196

THURSDAY
15
193
1½ mile - Hart House 17:14 (1/11:24)
2½ wk   10½ mo   15½ yr

FRIDAY
16
193

SATURDAY
17
St. Patrick's Day 192

Yvonne and Yvette share an inside joke.
Photograph by Jule Campbell.

MARCH

S	M	T	W	T	F	S
				1	2	3
4	5	6	7	8	9	10
11	12	13	14	15	16	17
18	19	20	21	22	23	24
25	26	27	28	29	30	31

SUNDAY 18
195   1:00
-2000 cal = 65050

MONDAY 19
192   1:30 = 2:30
-1250 = 3250 = 66300 (18.9)

TUESDAY 20
1½ m Hart House 17:23 (1m in 11:31)
193 lbs   1:33 = 4:03
-1000 cal = 4250 = 67300
12m/mo   17 yr

WEDNESDAY 21
191 lbs
2m Hart House 22:48   14/mo/19yr

THURSDAY 22

FRIDAY 23

SATURDAY 24

Sneaking up on Kara.
Photograph by Marc Hispard.

MARCH

S	M	T	W	T	F	S
				1	2	3
4	5	6	7	8	9	10
11	12	13	14	15	16	17
18	19	20	21	22	23	24
25	26	27	28	29	30	31

SUNDAY

25

MONDAY

26

TUESDAY

27

190 lbs
2 m Hart House in 21:56 1 m 10:59 pushing at end.
walk to subway.   16/mo 21 yr

WEDNESDAY

28

189 lbs   2 m River   25:37   12: to Culvert
          18 mo   27/yr

THURSDAY

29

FRIDAY

30

187 lbs 2 m H.H. 120 mo 25 yr
         22:59

SATURDAY

31

Kathy steals the scene from wild mustangs along a Cabo San Lucas beach.

Photograph by Paolo Curto.

APRIL

S M T W T F S
1 2 3 4 5 6 7
8 9 10 11 12 13 14
15 16 17 18 19 20 21
22 23 24 25 26 27 28
29 30

SUNDAY
1

188 lbs   19.4 % Body Fat
2m - river 25:05 rest at 1 & 1½

MONDAY
2

TUESDAY
3

WEDNESDAY
4

THURSDAY
5

FRIDAY
6

SATURDAY
7

Maria looks peachy in a one-shoulder maillot at Costa Careyes, Mexico.
Photograph by Marc Hispard.

APRIL

S M T W T F S
1 2 3 4 5 6 7
8 9 10 11 12 13 14
15 16 17 18 19 20 21
22 23 24 25 26 27 28
29 30

SUNDAY *Palm Sunday*

8

MONDAY

9

TUESDAY *Passover* 1 8 6

10 1½ m H.H. 18:12 (1m 11:59)

WEDNESDAY

11

THURSDAY 185 ½ river 19:29 3/wk/5m. 30 ys

12

FRIDAY *Good Friday* 186 14.63K - River - Scarlett - Jane 15.1 Avg 31.7 M

13 57.58
walk to footbridge with Sue.

SATURDAY 187 lunch at Housey in St. Catherine.

14

Things are looking up for Elle.

Photograph by Jay Maisel.

APRIL

S	M	T	W	T	F	S
1	2	3	4	5	6	7
8	9	10	11	12	13	14
15	16	17	18	19	20	21
22	23	24	25	26	27	28
29	30					

SUNDAY
15
Easter Sunday 188   2 m 7/mo 32/yr   River 48° 23:33 R.T.
5 min rest at 1 mile - 2 at 1½ ran hill.

MONDAY
16
188   19.71K to school 17.5 Avg 44 Mx 1:07:20 (31:59 to school)
34.6 mo

TUESDAY
17
188   20.13K to Sch 17.5 Avg 38.4 Mx 54.8 yr 1:08:58

WEDNESDAY
18

THURSDAY
19

FRIDAY
20

SATURDAY
21

Kelly and Kathy boppin' on the beach

Photograph by Paolo Curto

APRIL

	S	M	T	W	T	F	S
	1	2	3	4	5	6	7
	8	9	10	11	12	13	14
	15	16	17	18	19	20	21
	22	23	24	25	26	27	28
	29	30					

SUNDAY

22

MONDAY

23

TUESDAY

24

WEDNESDAY

25

THURSDAY

26

FRIDAY

27

190 lbs — 26.04K to school, Clarke Henning – home by lake
17.5 Avg   37.8 MX   81.8 mo   1:29:18

SATURDAY

28

188 lbs — 2.24K to Hardware Store
13.7 Avg   49.9 MX   84.1 mo   9:49

Elle takes flight on Australia's Great Barrier Reef.

Photograph by Jay Maisel.

APRIL / MAY

S	M	T	W	T	F	S
		1	2	3	4	5
6	7	8	9	10	11	12
13	14	15	16	17	18	19
20	21	22	23	24	25	26
27	28	29	30	31		

SUNDAY
29

186   70.42 K   17.6 Avg   47.5 Mx   154.9 mo   3:59:31
Bike a Thon - Old Mill & Humber Bay, plus Leslie
Street Spit.

MONDAY
30

TUESDAY
1

WEDNESDAY
2

THURSDAY
3

198 lbs   23.15 to Sch & CAA   15.7 Avg   38.7 Mx
178.2 yr   1:28:28

FRIDAY
4

195 lbs

SATURDAY
5

Rachel will do in a pinch.

Photograph by Ann Gallagher.

MAY

S M T W T F S
1 2 3 4 5
6 7 8 9 10 11 12
13 14 15 16 17 18 19
20 21 22 23 24 25 26
27 28 29 30 31

SUNDAY

6

MONDAY

7

TUESDAY

8

WEDNESDAY

9

THURSDAY

10

FRIDAY

11

SATURDAY

12

Playing ball with Ashley.

Photograph by Marc Hispard.

May

S M T W T F S
1 2 3 4 5
6 7 8 9 10 11 12
13 14 15 16 17 18 19
20 21 22 23 24 25 26
27 28 29 30 31

Sunday	*Mother's Day*
13	

Monday	185 lbs 20.02K to school 17.7 Avg 47.5 mx 198.4 yr 1:07
14	

Tuesday	
15	

Wednesday	
16	

Thursday	
17	

Friday	185 1m - river 12:37 5:48 to ridge - rest 2/5 hill
18	

Saturday	*Armed Forces Day* 194
19	

A sun-kissed Kara seeks the shade.
Photograph by Marc Hispard.

MAY

S M T W T F S
1 2 3 4 5
6 7 8 9 10 11 12
13 14 15 16 17 18 19
20 21 22 23 24 25 26
27 28 29 30 31

SUNDAY
20
185

MONDAY
21
Victoria Day (Canada)   187   7.44 K   From Roncesvalles auto
15.5 Avg   37.9 MX   205.8 yr   28:40

TUESDAY
22
188   15.7 K to school & Roncesvalles
18.6 Avg   37.2 MX   221.7 yr   50:35

WEDNESDAY
23
184   19.54 K to school   17.7 Avg   43.1 MX
241.3 yr   1:06:07   42.68 WK   85.85 mo

THURSDAY
24
185

FRIDAY
25
185   1m   12:54   rest at ½

SATURDAY
26
185   1m   13:24 rest at ½
2 wk
6.9 K to W E H H c   15.4 Avg   35.3 MX   248.4 yr   26:48
92.75 mo

Stephanie gives Marc some advice.
Photograph by Ann Gallagher.

MAY/JUNE

S M T W T F S
1 2
3 4 5 6 7 8 9
10 11 12 13 14 15 16
17 18 19 20 21 22 23
24 25 26 27 28 29 30

SUNDAY
27
184 1½ m 18:25 5:55 ridge ⊡-¾-9:00 rest - by
river on return - ⅗ hill
4½ rao

MONDAY *Memorial Day (Observed)* 185 1½ m 17:29 5:32 ridge 8:31 ¾ rest
⅗ hill
3 wk - 6 mo 38 yr

TUESDAY
29
187 (Hannaford Banquet

WEDNESDAY *Memorial Day* 185 1½ m - noon 18:32 ¾ 8:06 back along
30
river, non-stop, except 2-3 minutes to loo
at cranes? & chat. medium upper body work

THURSDAY
31
184 1½ m - non stop ¾ in 8:30 - back along
river. 19:43
6 wk - 9 mo - 41 yr

FRIDAY
1

SATURDAY
2

Sylvanders come in two colors.
Photograph by Robert Huntzinger.

JUNE

SUNDAY

3

MONDAY

4

TUESDAY

5

WEDNESDAY

6

1 mile run - 42 yr

THURSDAY

7

FRIDAY

8

SATURDAY

9

Lovely Elle casts a spell.

Photograph by Jay Maisel.

JUNE

S	M	T	W	T	F	S
					1	2
3	4	5	6	7	8	9
10	11	12	13	14	15	16
17	18	19	20	21	22	23
24	25	26	27	28	29	30

SUNDAY

10

MONDAY

11

TUESDAY

12

WEDNESDAY

13

THURSDAY *Flag Day*   58.76 K   310.24 r

14

FRIDAY   2.85 K

15

SATURDAY   46 32 K   359.84 r   107.93 w K

16

Christie on a windswept beach at Manda Island off the Kenya coast.

Photograph by John G. Zimmerman

JUNE

S M T W T F S
                1 2
3 4 5 6 7 8 9
10 11 12 13 14 15 16
17 18 19 20 21 22 23
24 25 26 27 28 29 30

SUNDAY *Father's Day*   80+ K   87.5 K

17

MONDAY   41, 25 K

18

TUESDAY   32.37 K

19

WEDNESDAY   62. 24 K

20

THURSDAY   36. 31 K   367.6 Trip   619.0 yr.   259.6 T w K
                                    and monTh

21

FRIDAY

22

SATURDAY

23

Kathy gets some help setting up

Photograph by Jule Campbell

JUNE

SUNDAY
24
188 lbs

MONDAY
25
188 lbs   2.51 K - twice up long hill - 621.5/yr

TUESDAY
26
187 lbs   5.16 K - 5 Halford loops 626.7/yr 22:51

WEDNESDAY
27
186 lbs   2.64 K   8:30 P.M - Halford loops trying
new freewheel. 629.3 yr.
10.31 wK

THURSDAY
28

FRIDAY
29

SATURDAY
30

La belle Estelle in jungle camouflage.
Photograph by Marc Hispard.

JULY

S M T W T F S
1 2 3 4 5 6 7
8 9 10 11 12 13 14
15 16 17 18 19 20 21
22 23 24 25 26 27 28
29 30 31

SUNDAY   *Canada Day (Canada)*

1

MONDAY

2

TUESDAY

3

WEDNESDAY   *Independence Day*

4

THURSDAY

5

FRIDAY

6

SATURDAY

7

Rachel and Maria are framed in a black and white sculpture along the Careyes coast.

Photograph by Marc Hispard.

July

S M T W T F S
1 2 3 4 5 6 7
8 9 10 11 12 13 14
15 16 17 18 19 20 21
22 23 24 25 26 27 28
29 30 31

SUNDAY

8

MONDAY

9

TUESDAY

10

WEDNESDAY

11

THURSDAY

12

FRIDAY

13

SATURDAY

14

Kara is cool by the pool.

Photograph by Marc Hispard.

JULY

S M T W T F S
1 2 3 4 5 6 7
8 9 10 11 12 13 14
15 16 17 18 19 20 21
22 23 24 25 26 27 28
29 30 31

SUNDAY

15

MONDAY

16

192 lbs

TUESDAY

17

194 lbs   9.43K   17.0Avg   47.1mx   1320.8yr   33:17
To Deborah, & 3 Hafford loops – upper
body weights.

WEDNESDAY

18

193 lbs

THURSDAY

19

191 lbs   5.60K – 5 long Hafford loops singles 13.1 Avg 1326.4 yr
25:38
1m, incl hill – 12:33   5 minutes or so
on rowing machine.

FRIDAY

20

189 lbs

SATURDAY

21

188 lbs   1 mile run – 12:05 non-stop
11.55K   19.3avg   37.1mx   1337.9yr   45:05
26.58wK

Rachel in a pensive moment.
Photograph by Marc Hispard.

July

S M T W T F S
1 2 3 4 5 6 7
8 9 10 11 12 13 14
15 16 17 18 19 20 21
22 23 24 25 26 27 28
29 30 31

SUNDAY
22
187 lbs - raining, tired - worked in basement.

MONDAY
23
198 lbs - 1 mile + run - 12:15 - from mile in path down dike today + back along river. One brief pause to look at kids fishing

TUESDAY
24
188 lbs 1 mile + run 12:14
8.82 K - 4 Halford hills + St. Marks
12.6 Avg 1346.8 yr 41:46
Fall weight workout.

WEDNESDAY
25
187 lbs - 4 mile walk to footbridge with Sue
1½ mile run - River, Halford, end of street
18:28 3½ m/wk 5½ mo 47½ yr

THURSDAY
26
187 lbs 20.09 K - to school 16.4 Avg (19 going) 1367.0 yr
1:13:15

FRIDAY
27
186

SATURDAY
28
189 1½ mile - river + Halford - dike - 5:39
18:22 5/wk 7 mo 49 yr

JULY/AUGUST

S M TW T F S
1 2 3 4
5 6 7 8 9 10 11
12 13 14 15 16 17 18
19 20 21 22 23 24 25
26 27 28 29 30 31

SUNDAY

29

188 lbs   1½ M- River + Halford   9:51 - Dike 5:30
8½ mo   5½ yr

MONDAY

30

186 lbs

TUESDAY

31

185   1½ mile - Hart House - 1 m - 10:48 rest ½ m 4:50 -
pushing it. 3 wk 10 mo 53 yr
22.59 K - to school 17.6 Avg 44.7 mx 1390.0 yr 1:16:52

WEDNESDAY

1

186   1 m - River - Dike (5:35) rest - heavy legs - 22" fast
11:56
5 K slowly - to check distances for running

THURSDAY

2

186   2 m River Dike 5:25) 1 m 10:30 150 P - rest 3-4 min 90
Trying to take long strides. Easier & by river on
return but 22" fast. 22:11
4½ wk - 3 mo 56 yr -
Full weights.

FRIDAY

3

186   2 m River - Dike 5:50+ 1 m 11:47 - 140 P - rest 4½ min 90 P in
3 minute 24:38 RT - felt tired - 6½ wk 5 mo 58 yr.

SATURDAY

4

AUGUST

S	M	T	W	T	F	S
				1	2	3	4
5	6	7	8	9	10	11
12	13	14	15	16	17	18
19	20	21	22	23	24	25
26	27	28	29	30	31

SUNDAY

5

185 1m river + dike (5:50+) - 12:15 20" sprint
6 mo 59 yr

MONDAY

6

184 2 m - river 22:41 dike 5:32 1m - 11:00 140P 100P after
2 minutes - 4 min rest :20 sprint on return.
3 wk 8 mo 61 yr.
12.01 K - High Park, Forcevalles with Sue - easy
12.7 Avr 140 8.8 yr 58:26

TUESDAY

7

184 1m river + dyke (5:12)(½ m - 5:09) :20 sprint - 11:10 TT
4 wk 8 mo 62 yr

WEDNESDAY

8

184 2 m - 1 around block with Sue - 11:24 - then river + dyke
½ m - 5:00 dyke 5:10 hill :26 :20 sprint 11:23
6 wk 10 mo 63 yr.

THURSDAY

9

183 1m - river + dyke - 4 P.M - heavy, tired ½ m - 6:00 rest
at dam, ⅗ hill. 13:22 RT
7 wk 11 mo 64 yr.

FRIDAY

10

183 2 m river - noon - 1 - 11:30 short walk with Cathy &
return - warm - no energy - 24:16
8 wk 12 mo 66 yr.

SATURDAY

11

182

AUGUST

S	M	T	W	T	F	S
			1	2	3	4
5	6	7	8	9	10	11
12	13	14	15	16	17	18
19	20	21	22	23	24	25
26	27	28	29	30	31	

SUNDAY
12 — 183

MONDAY
13 — 181

TUESDAY
14 — 182 lbs   1½ mile river with Sue & Cathy - Dyke 6:00
:20 sprint - hard hill   14½ mo   65½ yr.

WEDNESDAY
15 — 181 lbs   1½ mile river with Sue - 4 walks - hard hill
3 wk 16 mo 67 yr.

THURSDAY
16

FRIDAY
17 — 3.96 K checking jogging path (14 12.8 yr)

SATURDAY
18 — 5.91 K - to classes   14 18.8 yr
9.87 wk 26.88 mo

Let's go, Mets! Let's go, Maria.
Photograph by Christine Walker

AUGUST

S	M	T	W	T	F	S
				1	2	3	4
5	6	7	8	9	10	11
12	13	14	15	16	17	18
19	20	21	22	23	24	25
26	27	28	29	30	31	

SUNDAY

19

2.4 K around camp 14 21.3 yr
29. 28 mo

MONDAY

20

43.59 - beyond Cooper's Falls 22.6 avg 52.5 mx
1465.0 yr 1:55:41
2.07 K to barn

TUESDAY

21

4.11 camp

WEDNESDAY

22

2.44 K camp 1473.7 yr
32.19 K Sealright Road & #169 24.3 Avg 51.3 MX 1505.9 yr
1.1 + .93 camp 88.83 w-K 115.71 mo 1:19:15

THURSDAY

23

42.86 K - with Sue - past Cooper's Falls
19.1 Avg 51.0 Mx 1550.9 yr 2:14:32 142 camp

FRIDAY

24

81.38 K - to Uphill 23.6 Avg 47.9 mx 1632.3 yr
3:26:17

SATURDAY

25

A colorfully suited Carol is picture perfect along the Maui coast
Photograph by Walter Iooss Jr

AUGUST/SEPTEMBER

SUNDAY
26

3.78K Camp   1636.2yr

MONDAY
27

3.75K   1640 yr

TUESDAY
28

1.99 K camp
26.48K - south of atterly 22.7 Avg 45.0 MX (40.6 on level
road) - 1668.5 yr 1:10:07
1.5M - Geneva loop 20:22 - heavy & stiff
5+ lengths swimming   17½ august 68½ per run

WEDNESDAY
29

9.24 K Camp   1677.9yr 36:05
1.5M Geneva loop 19:01

THURSDAY
30

1.5M Geneva loop 19:01 swim along shore. 19mo/70ff
17.22 - Old Grist Mill   29.4 Avg 49.1 MX 1695.24
4.23K camp   39:05
                        1699.54r

FRIDAY
31

2.24 K camp
43.34 Hwag 13 northwest of washago 21.9 Avg 46.4 MX
       1745.2 yr 1:58:27
3.14 camp   1748.4 yr

SATURDAY
1

1.95 camp   1750.4 yr   (341.6 camp)

SEPTEMBER

SUNDAY
2

MONDAY — *Labor Day*
3
24.65K to school & CNE   16.1 Avg   1775.5/yr
26.6/mo

TUESDAY
4
19.85K to school   17.5Avg   1795.5 yr   1:07:58

WEDNESDAY
5

THURSDAY
6

FRIDAY
7

SATURDAY
8

Rachel takes five.
Photograph by Jule Campbell.

SEPTEMBER

SUNDAY

9

163.50 K with TBN to St. George   21.9 Avg 52.9 Max 1959.1 yr
7:22:03 (½ way - 82.5 K 24.2 Avg 3:24:16)
4:02:47 returning   Left 9:12 AM - return 6:37 - 9:25 total time

MONDAY

10

TUESDAY

11

WEDNESDAY

12

19.65 K to school   19.8 Avg 48.5 Mx   1978.9 yr   59:29

THURSDAY

13

FRIDAY

14

SATURDAY

15

Estelle sends a message.
Photograph by Christine Walker.

SEPTEMBER

SUNDAY

16

180 - 1mile P.M - river - with Sue - many stops
creaky knees.

MONDAY

17

180   1M A.M. River   2:53 path 5:35 dyke, 11:56 R:
rest at dam.

TUESDAY

18

180

WEDNESDAY

19

179   1M A.M. - on path 5:48 D:Ke - 12:28 non-stop
3/wk & month   73 year

THURSDAY

20

Rosh Hashanah

FRIDAY

21

SATURDAY

22

Kara takes a stroll on the surf side.
Photograph by Marc Hispard.

SEPTEMBER

SUNDAY

23

MONDAY

24

TUESDAY

25

WEDNESDAY

26

THURSDAY

27

FRIDAY

28

SATURDAY   *Yom Kippur*

29

Rachel hams it up

Photograph by Ann Gallagher

SEPTEMBER/OCTOBER

S	M	T	W	T	F	
	1	2	3	4	5	(
7	8	9	10	11	12	13
14	15	16	17	18	19	20
21	22	23	24	25	26	27
28	29	30	31			

SUNDAY
30

MONDAY
1

TUESDAY
2

WEDNESDAY
3

THURSDAY
4

FRIDAY
5

SATURDAY
6

Christie plays it safe while checking the local wildlife.

Photograph by John G. Zimmerman.

OCTOBER

S	M	T	W	T	F	S
	1	2	3	4	5	6
7	8	9	10	11	12	13
14	15	16	17	18	19	20
21	22	23	24	25	26	27
28	29	30	31			

SUNDAY
7

MONDAY   *Columbus Day (Observed)*   *Thanksgiving Day (Canada)*
8

TUESDAY
9

WEDNESDAY
10

THURSDAY
11

FRIDAY   *Columbus Day*
12

SATURDAY
13

Maria waits patiently.

Photograph by Marc Hispard.

OCTOBER

S	M	T	W	T	F	S
		1	2	3	4	5	6
7	8	9	10	11	12	13
14	15	16	17	18	19	20
21	22	23	24	25	26	27
28	29	30	31			

SUNDAY
14

MONDAY
15

TUESDAY
16

WEDNESDAY
17

THURSDAY
18

FRIDAY
19

SATURDAY
20

182 lbs - 1 m - river 4:30 P M - walk - rest at dam, ½ hr
dyke 6:10, 13:10 moving time.
1/mo 74 year

Tag-team champs Yvette and Yvonne.
Photograph by Robert Huntzinger.

OCTOBER

S	M	T	W	T	F	S
	1	2	3	4	5	6
7	8	9	10	11	12	13
14	15	16	17	18	19	20
21	22	23	24	25	26	27
28	29	30	31			

SUNDAY

21

MONDAY

22

TUESDAY

23

WEDNESDAY

24

THURSDAY

25

FRIDAY

26

SATURDAY

27

Kathy on the heights at Cabo San Lucas.

Photograph by Jule Campbell.

OCTOBER/NOVEMBER

S	M	T	W	T	F	S
				1	2	3
4	5	6	7	8	9	10
11	12	13	14	15	16	17
18	19	20	21	22	23	24
25	26	27	28	29	30	

SUNDAY

28

MONDAY

29

TUESDAY

30

WEDNESDAY   *Halloween*

31

THURSDAY

1

FRIDAY

2

SATURDAY

3

Ashley high above a calm sea at the Camino Real in Ixtapa.

Photograph by Christine Walker.

November

S M T W T F S
       1 2 3
4 5 6 7 8 9 10
11 12 13 14 15 16 17
18 19 20 21 22 23 24
25 26 27 28 29 30

SUNDAY

4

MONDAY

5

TUESDAY   *Election Day*

6

WEDNESDAY

7

THURSDAY

8

FRIDAY

9

SATURDAY

10

¡Olé! Rachel

Photograph by Marc Hispard

NOVEMBER

S M T W T F S
          1 2 3
4 5 6 7 8 9 10
11 12 13 14 15 16 17
18 19 20 21 22 23 24
25 26 27 28 29 30

SUNDAY   *Veterans Day*

11

MONDAY

12

TUESDAY

13

WEDNESDAY

14

THURSDAY

15

19.48K to school   17.2 Avg   36.9 MX
1998.4 yr   1:07:44

FRIDAY

16

SATURDAY

17

Kathy between takes
Photograph by Jule Campbell

November

SUNDAY

18

MONDAY

19

TUESDAY

20

WEDNESDAY

21

THURSDAY   *Thanksgiving Day*

22

FRIDAY

23

SATURDAY

24

Elle takes the bou

Photograph by Jay Maise

November / December

S M T W T F S

2 3 4 5 6 7 8
9 10 11 12 13 14 15
16 17 18 19 20 21 22
23 24 25 26 27 28 29
30 31

SUNDAY
25

MONDAY
26

TUESDAY
27

WEDNESDAY
28

THURSDAY
29

FRIDAY
30

SATURDAY
1

Lake Powell sculpture with Yvonne

Photograph by Robert Huntzinger

December

S M T W T F
2 3 4 5 6 7
9 10 11 12 13 14
16 17 18 19 20 21
23 24 25 26 27 28
30 31

SUNDAY

2

MONDAY

3

TUESDAY

4

WEDNESDAY

5

THURSDAY

6

FRIDAY

7

SATURDAY

8

Rachel, just a little bit blue
Photograph by Marc Hispar

December

S M T W T F S
1
2 3 4 5 6 7 8
9 10 11 12 13 14 15
16 17 18 19 20 21 22
23 24 25 26 27 28 29
30 31

SUNDAY

9

MONDAY

10

TUESDAY

11

WEDNESDAY   *Hanukkah*

12

THURSDAY

13

FRIDAY

14

SATURDAY

15

Only a touch-up for Maria

Photograph by Ann Gallagher

DECEMBER

S M T W T F S
1
2 3 4 5 6 7 8
9 10 11 12 13 14 15
16 17 18 19 20 21 22
23 24 25 26 27 28 29
30 31

SUNDAY
16

MONDAY
17

TUESDAY
18

WEDNESDAY
19

THURSDAY
20

FRIDAY
21

SATURDAY
22

Stephanie south of the border in Las Hadas.

Photograph by Marc Hispard.

December

S M T W T F S
2 3 4 5 6 7 8
9 10 11 12 13 14 15
16 17 18 19 20 21 22
23 24 25 26 27 28 29
30 31

SUNDAY

23

MONDAY

24

TUESDAY   *Christmas Day*

25

WEDNESDAY

26

THURSDAY

27

FRIDAY

28

SATURDAY

29

Having an Elle of a time in the surf.

Photograph by Jay Maisel.

DECEMBER / JANUARY

S	M	T	W	T	F
		1	2	3	4
6	7	8	9	10	11	1
13	14	15	16	17	18	1
20	21	22	23	24	25	2
27	28	29	30	31	

SUNDAY

30

MONDAY

31

TUESDAY   *New Year's Day*

1

WEDNESDAY

2

THURSDAY

3

FRIDAY

4

SATURDAY

5

NOTES

NOTES

1989

JANUARY
S	M	T	W	T	F	S
1	2	3	4	5	6	7
8	9	10	11	12	13	14
15	16	17	18	19	20	21
22	23	24	25	26	27	28
29	30	31				

FEBRUARY
S	M	T	W	T	F	S
			1	2	3	4
5	6	7	8	9	10	11
12	13	14	15	16	17	18
19	20	21	22	23	24	25
26	27	28				

MARCH
S	M	T	W	T	F	S
			1	2	3	4
5	6	7	8	9	10	11
12	13	14	15	16	17	18
19	20	21	22	23	24	25
26	27	28	29	30	31	

APRIL
S	M	T	W	T	F	S
						1
2	3	4	5	6	7	8
9	10	11	12	13	14	15
16	17	18	19	20	21	22
23	24	25	26	27	28	29
30						

MAY
S	M	T	W	T	F	S
	1	2	3	4	5	6
7	8	9	10	11	12	13
14	15	16	17	18	19	20
21	22	23	24	25	26	27
28	29	30	31			

JUNE
S	M	T	W	T	F
				1	2
4	5	6	7	8	9
11	12	13	14	15	16
18	19	20	21	22	23
25	26	27	28	29	30

JULY
S	M	T	W	T	F	S
						1
2	3	4	5	6	7	8
9	10	11	12	13	14	15
16	17	18	19	20	21	22
23	24	25	26	27	28	29
30	31					

AUGUST
S	M	T	W	T	F	S
		1	2	3	4	5
6	7	8	9	10	11	12
13	14	15	16	17	18	19
20	21	22	23	24	25	26
27	28	29	30	31		

SEPTEMBER
S	M	T	W	T	F	S
					1	2
3	4	5	6	7	8	9
10	11	12	13	14	15	16
17	18	19	20	21	22	23
24	25	26	27	28	29	30

OCTOBER
S	M	T	W	T	F	S
1	2	3	4	5	6	7
8	9	10	11	12	13	14
15	16	17	18	19	20	21
22	23	24	25	26	27	28
29	30	31				

NOVEMBER
S	M	T	W	T	F	S
			1	2	3	4
5	6	7	8	9	10	11
12	13	14	15	16	17	18
19	20	21	22	23	24	25
26	27	28	29	30		

DECEMBER
S	M	T	W	T	F
					1
3	4	5	6	7	8
10	11	12	13	14	15
17	18	19	20	21	22
24	25	26	27	28	29
31					

1990

JANUARY
S	M	T	W	T	F	S
	1	2	3	4	5	6
7	8	9	10	11	12	13
14	15	16	17	18	19	20
21	22	23	24	25	26	27
28	29	30	31			

FEBRUARY
S	M	T	W	T	F	S
				1	2	3
4	5	6	7	8	9	10
11	12	13	14	15	16	17
18	19	20	21	22	23	24
25	26	27	28			

MARCH
S	M	T	W	T	F	S
				1	2	3
4	5	6	7	8	9	10
11	12	13	14	15	16	17
18	19	20	21	22	23	24
25	26	27	28	29	30	31

APRIL
S	M	T	W	T	F	S
1	2	3	4	5	6	7
8	9	10	11	12	13	14
15	16	17	18	19	20	21
22	23	24	25	26	27	28
29	30					

MAY
S	M	T	W	T	F	S
		1	2	3	4	5
6	7	8	9	10	11	12
13	14	15	16	17	18	19
20	21	22	23	24	25	26
27	28	29	30	31		

JUNE
S	M	T	W	T	F
					1
3	4	5	6	7	8
10	11	12	13	14	15
17	18	19	20	21	22
24	25	26	27	28	29

JULY
S	M	T	W	T	F	S
1	2	3	4	5	6	7
8	9	10	11	12	13	14
15	16	17	18	19	20	21
22	23	24	25	26	27	28
29	30	31				

AUGUST
S	M	T	W	T	F	S
			1	2	3	4
5	6	7	8	9	10	11
12	13	14	15	16	17	18
19	20	21	22	23	24	25
26	27	28	29	30	31	

SEPTEMBER
S	M	T	W	T	F	S
						1
2	3	4	5	6	7	8
9	10	11	12	13	14	15
16	17	18	19	20	21	22
23	24	25	26	27	28	29
30						

OCTOBER
S	M	T	W	T	F	S
	1	2	3	4	5	6
7	8	9	10	11	12	13
14	15	16	17	18	19	20
21	22	23	24	25	26	27
28	29	30	31			

NOVEMBER
S	M	T	W	T	F	S
				1	2	3
4	5	6	7	8	9	10
11	12	13	14	15	16	17
18	19	20	21	22	23	24
25	26	27	28	29	30	

DECEMBER
S	M	T	W	T	F
2	3	4	5	6	7
9	10	11	12	13	14
16	17	18	19	20	21
23	24	25	26	27	28
30	31				

1991

JANUARY
S	M	T	W	T	F	S
		1	2	3	4	5
6	7	8	9	10	11	12
13	14	15	16	17	18	19
20	21	22	23	24	25	26
27	28	29	30	31		

FEBRUARY
S	M	T	W	T	F	S
					1	2
3	4	5	6	7	8	9
10	11	12	13	14	15	16
17	18	19	20	21	22	23
24	25	26	27	28		

MARCH
S	M	T	W	T	F	S
					1	2
3	4	5	6	7	8	9
10	11	12	13	14	15	16
17	18	19	20	21	22	23
24	25	26	27	28	29	30
31						

APRIL
S	M	T	W	T	F	S
	1	2	3	4	5	6
7	8	9	10	11	12	13
14	15	16	17	18	19	20
21	22	23	24	25	26	27
28	29	30				

MAY
S	M	T	W	T	F	S
			1	2	3	4
5	6	7	8	9	10	11
12	13	14	15	16	17	18
19	20	21	22	23	24	25
26	27	28	29	30	31	

JUNE
S	M	T	W	T	F
2	3	4	5	6	7
9	10	11	12	13	14
16	17	18	19	20	21
23	24	25	26	27	28
30					

JULY
S	M	T	W	T	F	S
	1	2	3	4	5	6
7	8	9	10	11	12	13
14	15	16	17	18	19	20
21	22	23	24	25	26	27
28	29	30	31			

AUGUST
S	M	T	W	T	F	S
				1	2	3
4	5	6	7	8	9	10
11	12	13	14	15	16	17
18	19	20	21	22	23	24
25	26	27	28	29	30	31

SEPTEMBER
S	M	T	W	T	F	S
1	2	3	4	5	6	7
8	9	10	11	12	13	14
15	16	17	18	19	20	21
22	23	24	25	26	27	28
29	30					

OCTOBER
S	M	T	W	T	F	S
		1	2	3	4	5
6	7	8	9	10	11	12
13	14	15	16	17	18	19
20	21	22	23	24	25	26
27	28	29	30	31		

NOVEMBER
S	M	T	W	T	F	S
					1	2
3	4	5	6	7	8	9
10	11	12	13	14	15	16
17	18	19	20	21	22	23
24	25	26	27	28	29	30

DECEMBER
S	M	T	W	T	F
1	2	3	4	5	6
8	9	10	11	12	13
15	16	17	18	19	20
22	23	24	25	26	27
29	30	31			